Up the Downs!

*A runner's celebration
of the Sussex hills*

Jack Arscott

GW00724550

You came and looked and loved the view
Long known and loved by me,
Green Sussex fading into blue
With one grey glimpse of sea.

Alfred, Lord Tennyson

Copyright © Jack Arscott 2018

Front cover photograph: Ashcombe Windmill, near Lewes, looking up to
    Kingston Ridge
Title page: Mount Caburn from Glynde

ISBN: 978-1-907242-70-0

Published by Pomegranate Press
South Chailey, Lewes, Sussex BN8 4QB
www. pomegranate-press.co.uk

Printed by 4Edge, Eldon Way, Hockley, Essex SS5 4AD

Contents

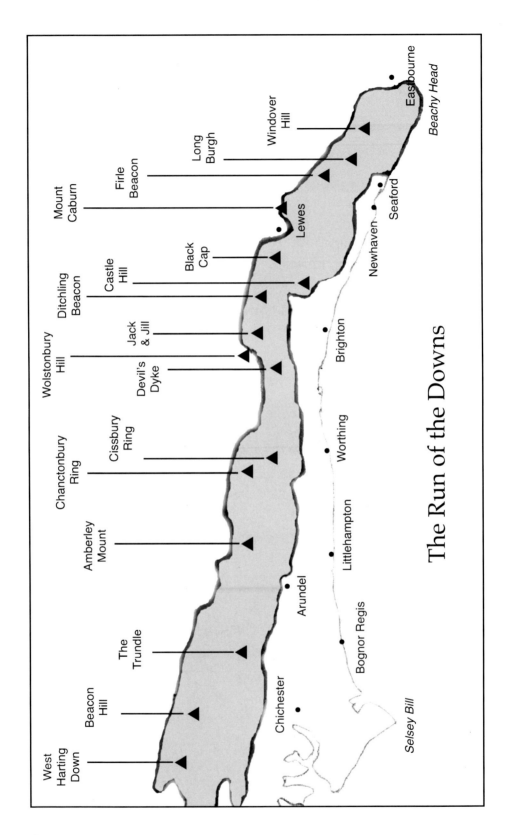

The Run of the Downs

Foreword

By Ash Head, co-founder of The Moyleman

Slipped out for a cheeky five miler over the rain-drenched hills before breakfast. After all the recent chirp about the joys of barefoot running, I strapped on my Vibram off-roaders for some greasy Five Fingers action.

I got more than I'd bargained for. The trails were treacherous, laced with mud and wet flint. The grass, whilst soft and yielding, was homicidally slick, the slightest camber offering a chance to slide into a hedgerow or slip in one of the large and plentiful cowpats.

Barefoot running on days like this ... pure joy. Even an ox like me can feel light and fast, running on quick, lively feet, mindful not to heel strike lest I impale a plate on a hidden shard of chalky rock.

Ash Head (left) with the late Chris Moyle.

The thin veil of cloud shrouding the Downs became a thick blanket on the summits. Large shapes loomed out of the Blackcap mist, cattle munching silently on juicy, wet grass.

I wrote this on a running forum some while ago, but it could have been yesterday. Or tomorrow. The Downs are timeless guardians of our towns, sleeping giants with whom we enjoy an ancient tryst. I like to think the love is requited: indeed, I'm certain of it. Ghosts of runners past whisper on the wind, guide us through the twists and turns, over flint and field.

These hills, these Downs, are a true national treasure. It is our privilege to venture out, to thrill our very souls in their embrace.

Adorned in autumn finery or shimmering in summer's sun, serenaded by spring lambs or blasted by cruel winter winds, these hills wait for us, patient, life-affirming, splendid.

In *Up The Downs!* Jack Arscott takes us on a personal journey along his favourite trails. You'll learn of landmarks, of lore, of places we Sussex hill-folk hold in our hearts. His tales are at once familiar and enlightening. They reflect our thoughts and feelings; they speak of friends; they share our passion and our joy.

Enjoy this book. Better yet, read it, then come and join us – for, dear trail-runner, here be paradise.

Ash Head

Introduction

The Weald is good, the Downs are best –
I'll give you the run of 'em east to west . . .

Rudyard Kipling: *The Run of the Downs*

The house I grew up in, near the war memorial in Lewes, looked out over Firle Beacon.

Every morning without fail, my dad would draw the blinds and greet those oh-so-distant hills with the words 'Good morning, Downs!' It seemed an eccentric ritual – and it was one that failed to resonate with me until long after the developers moved in down the road, flattened the old printworks and threw up a jungle of flats that partially obscured the view.

In the summer of 2016, I returned home from university and learned the error of my ways. I had become reasonably well-travelled over the course of a four-year modern languages degree, but it didn't take me long to realise I had been missing something. That something was elemental, revelatory and just waiting to be discovered.

Sure, my family went on the occasional excursion to the top of the Downs – anywhere with an ice cream van was the general idea – and the first eighteen years of my life had played out largely in their shadow. From our first house in Westmeston, we could virtually have flown a paper plane up to Ditchling Beacon had we wanted to.

But my enjoyment of the landscape I have come to cherish had been chiefly a passive one. The golf course at the top of Chapel Hill was visible from the terraces of the Dripping Pan, where my dad and I still watch our beloved football team, and I have fond memories of a picnic on Malling Down surrounded by a herd of hungry goats. There my reminiscences stopped.

So it was curiosity, rather than force of habit, that prompted me to lace up my shoes and venture into the hills that summer. So vital have the Downs become to my sense of self that it is hard to recreate what I felt that first time. All I know looking back is that I spent the happiest summer of my young life scampering around a paradise of greenery, engaged perhaps in sloughing off all the accumulated cares of a relentless and demanding decade of study.

That, I now know, is the paradox of hill running. Much as your happiness can come to depend on it, it remains an act of abandonment; an out-of-body experience; a tribute to the land beneath our feet. To the uninitiated this will sound like so much mythologising, but talk to anyone who does it and they will confirm the emotional connection binding them to their natural 'playground'.

I moved to Germany in the autumn to take up my first job since graduating. On my last run before flying out, I set off from our present house in South Chailey and scaled the northern flank of Black Cap, before skirting the top of Mount Harry and cantering down through Landport Bottom en route to Lewes. As I looked up at Kingston Ridge and let my gaze travel as far as the pylons over Firle, I realised there was a lump in my throat. Before I knew it, I was bidding a silent farewell to the hills and vowing to come back and run them again when I could.

That chance came sooner than planned. With the job failing to live up to expectations, I returned to Sussex to train as a journalist – and renew my frustrated love affair. It is a strange relationship, equal parts pain and transcendent joy, but it is one that never fails to lift my spirits. Since that summer the landscape has opened up and revealed hitherto unknown routes (many featured in this book), teaching me valuable lessons in resilience and consolidating that sense of oneness between man and nature I had once thought the preserve of hippies.

In early 2018 I took the train from Lewes to Eastbourne with the idea of running back along the South Downs Way to Firle Beacon. In that giddy first summer, I had taken the same route with rather different results. Disorientated, dog-tired and wary of dwindling public transport opportunities at that time of the evening, I had ended in Alfriston. But this time I was confident of my bearings. Instead of confusing my internal compass, the westward journey from the eastern end of the South Downs range at Beachy Head joined the dots on the mental map I had been unconsciously assembling since coming home.

It now seems a perfectly logical place for our journey to begin.

Jack Arscott

The Long Man of Wilmington. Along Windover Hill we run over his head!

Hikers and mountain bikers

Beachy Head – Firle Beacon
14 miles

First, a confession: this run doesn't actually start at Beachy Head. Not unless you really want it to, anyway. Not having a car, I came into Eastbourne by train, meaning my starting point was actually the railway station.

But at least it gave me a proper run-up for the ascent of Beachy Head – a luxury not afforded those tackling the marathon of the same name. At the top, I was faced with a dilemma: follow the coast road round to Birling Gap and cut inland from there, or stick to the South Downs Way and hug the ridge until the pylons over Firle appear to light the way?

I chose the latter, and soon put the least attractive part of the route behind me. The Way shadows the road for a little while, until a track through Eastbourne Downs Golf Club offers a welcome escape. Apart from the slightly unnerving presence of busy golf links on either side of the path, this is a pleasant, rolling stretch with views of the sea to the port side and the Weald to starboard.

A mile or two further along the ridge, a trig point – adorned on the day I passed by with a memorial wreath – marks the start of a long descent into Jevington. Teeming with hikers and mountain bikers, this slope burrows down to the Ouse Valley floor with a single-mindedness lacking in any consideration for the gung-ho runner's ankles. Fortunately, I wasn't taking any chances.

After navigating a natural obstacle course through a tunnel of trees, I emerged onto the main drag through humble Jevington, passing the birthplace of my favourite pudding as I did so. The Hungry Monk pub inadvertently gave the world banoffee pie – or banoffi, as the blue plaque on the wall inexplicably calls it – before closing in 2012. But the sweetest accident ever recorded must remain a daydream, because there is a tough climb ahead of us.

Passing a stables on the left, the Way creeps up – almost tentatively at first – into the trees. Then it shrugs its shoulders and makes a break for it, streaking up the hillside as if impatient for the view at the top. At the summit, a right-hand turn into a field duly obliges with sweeping perspectives to Firle Beacon and beyond. In the immediate foreground, what is left of a dilapidated farmhouse is engaged in the painstaking act of crawling into the turf and oblivion.

At this point, the rest of the route is mapped out on the horizon. It may not look easy, exactly, but there is a comfort in knowing what lies ahead. Another headlong descent round the brow of Windover Hill and down into Alfriston forces us to surrender the high ground and the vantage point it provides, though the fleeting view below of the so-called Cathedral of the Downs (more modestly, St Andrew's parish church) goes some way towards making up for it.

The Way briefly crosses the Street road into Wilmington before completing its graceful fall into Alfriston. Across a water meadow, the church rears up on the other side of the expiring Cuckmere on its valedictory way to the Haven. Scorning the advances of the riverside path to the 'lost village' of Exceat – a fork of the Way in its own right – I edged across the high street and scaled Kings Ride towards Long Burgh, a good half a mile of up to leave the village far behind.

This was the last big heave of the day, with two undulating miles to the car park at Firle Beacon giving me ample opportunity to take stock of the miles I had covered since setting out from central Eastbourne earlier in the day.

As Seaford Head disappeared in my wing mirror, I was treading familiar ground at last. Away to the north-east, Mount Caburn saluted me like an old friend as I rode the wind all the way home to my second-favourite summit.

Mount Caburn, Lewes

3 – 6 miles

Strange though it may seem to dedicate a whole chapter to one hill, this one has a special place in my heart.

The first reason for this is quite simple: I know every blade of grass on it. Rising imposingly just east of my home town of Lewes, it can best be reached by way of Chapel Hill. Painters are often to be found on the bends of the latter, aiming their easels at the gap between the higgledy-piggledy houses through which the castle stands proud over an agreeable commotion of narrow streets. From up here, the county town appears in its best light.

The immaculately manicured golf course at the top of the hill gives way after a right turn to slightly more rugged terrain. Through the gate and past the cattle trough, the gentle synchronicity of the slowly falling fields on either side immediately arrests your attention. Then the frantic trill of the resident skylarks, advance guard of these hills, engages another of your senses.

The Ouse Valley from the summit of Caburn, with Itford Hill in the background.

By the time you reach the post that stands at a fork in the path, you can feast your eyes on an uninterrupted view of Caburn rushing inexorably skywards to the immediate south-east of you.

This orphaned gatepost is the clue to my second reason for loving this landscape, which is that it presents the runner with several possibilities. The most obvious route continues downhill on a narrow track emptying out into an uneven meadow surrounded by steep arable fields. The dew pond in Oxteddle Bottom prefaces Caburn itself, over a stile at the end of a gauntlet of thirsty cattle. The reward for the punishing climb to the well-camouflaged Iron Age hill fort is an only slightly less abrupt descent to the hallowed cricket green in the village of Glynde, sadly shorn now of the Trevor Arms pub.

Alternatively, you can turn left at the gatepost. The half-mile jog to the gate overlooking the controversial wind turbine at Glyndebourne invariably involves scattering a herd of sheep, but opera connoisseurs will prefer it for the short cut it offers to the concert hall on the long road out of the village. This is no idle whimsy: I once heard a guest singer in high season describing her

Cows are constant companions on the way from the golf course to Caburn.

ambulatory commute in dreamy terms to a couple at a neighbouring café table. The only thing she omitted to mention was the view of Firle Beacon about ten kilometres away, crowned with twin electricity pylons and a worthy destination for a challenging training run – see the following chapter for a more circuitous route.

The third option is also the third reason for my attachment to Mount Caburn. If you veer sharp left above the wind turbine – that gate is marked Southerham Nature Reserve – and double back on yourself, instead of dropping down the tussocky slope to Glyndebourne, you soon come to the perimeter fence of the golf course. Turn here and follow the fence round to the right so that you are facing the Ringmer road. Then, keeping the green on your left, follow the high path under scraggly trees until another gate appears across the field on your right about half a mile further on.

This is Malling Down, and there is no place quite like it. Buried in grassy craters that dominate Earwig Corner below, one of the rarest butterfly colonies in the country and the most fertile chalk grassland in the county cling to contours of prehistoric wonder. The untamed landscape in the shallow hollow to your right is vividly terrestrial and graphically lunar at the same time, a playful foil to the imperiously plunging slopes out of sight on your left.

Should you be in the mood for a detour, you could hug the golf course and take the lower path along the rim of the deeper of the two valleys. At the remotest corner of the golf course, a gate opens out onto a wide grass track running along the bottom of the hillside. Down the slope to your left, the mouth of Malling Down yawns expansively. Sheep and gorse run wild up its sides; in the narrow gulley at the valley bottom, diligent gardeners try to keep their allotments in check.

By all means, stop and stare by the gate overlooking the transfixingly gothic Undercliffe House – but don't be tempted to descend to the valley floor. Such paths as there are to street level owe their existence entirely to the soles of generations of intrepid walkers on the same foolhardy mission to subject nature to man's whim.

Instead, either swing to the right along the edge of Malling Hill as far as the next gate or retrace your steps up the hillside and back briefly into the golf course's orbit. If you choose the latter, you should then enter the valley you were admiring before curiosity got the better of you. Halfway down it on the far side, duck through a gate hidden in the undergrowth and follow the rudimentary path down to the right. In no time, you're back in a smaller version of the lunar landscape you've just left.

To regain the streets of Lewes, skitter down two flights of steps separated by a gate straight ahead of you. Turn left at the bottom and follow your nose all the way down to the Ringmer road, entering the slipstream of your alter ego as you go.

The humps and bumps of Malling Down nature reserve.

Heart Attack Hill

Moyleman first half (and a bit)
or Landport Bottom, Lewes – Firle Beacon
15 miles

Taking in some of the loftiest summits in the South Downs range, the Moyleman marathon circumnavigates the East Sussex county town of Lewes before tumbling down into Cliffe High Street in triumph. The annual event was thought up by Ash Head and named after his friend and running partner, Chris Moyle, who died of stomach cancer in 2009.

Since its inception in 2014 the course has begun in the long grass of Landport Bottom, found somewhat misleadingly above the prison and the sprawling Nevill estate at the top of town. Passing the largely disused racecourse after a gentle gambol through the fields, we find ourselves at the base of Black Cap. Electricity pylons stalk the horizon in a manner both unobtrusive and helpful for orienteering purposes.

In scaling the eastern slope of Black Cap, we are eschewing the shady allure of wooded Mount Harry over to the right. A brief detour would reveal one of the most photogenic views of the downland around Lewes, namely the open pastures and steep, cultivated farmland that unfurl towards Offham far below. Roughly halfway between this vantage point and the start line yawns a quarry, invisible to the Moyleman runner, from which waggons once ferried chalk through a tunnel on a vertiginous journey to the banks of the River Ouse at the valley bottom.

Enough of this. Having paid our respects to the haughty bracket at the top of the field, another extinguished star in the constellation of beacons by which long-gone coastguards were supposed to tip off the rest of the county in the event of invasion by sea, we have reached the trig point at the top of Black Cap. Instead of taking the path that runs all the way to the Jack and Jill windmills over Clayton, we are going to entrust our ankles to the narrow track to Housedean Farm.

At this stage, the Sussex Weald materialises on our left. Rippling away in the direction of the Ouse Valley in flickering shades of green and gold, the crop fields burst irregularly into clouds of birds. These creatures are your mascots for over a mile, until an apparently harmless copse swallows you up. In fact, these trees are home to Heart Attack Hill, one of the Moyleman's hushed landmarks. This is a breathless scramble up a near vertical slope, bringing you out onto the crest of the brow overlooking the distinctly unlovely A27.

After a perilously abrupt drop down to the dual carriageway, you can console yourself with the thought that you have a quarter of the journey behind you – or, in our case, almost half a half marathon ('a sensible distance', the course record holder kindly told my younger self on one occasion). Encouraging though these numbers may be, however, you ain't done nothing yet.

The trig point at Black Cap, with a view of the old Lewes Racecourse in the distance.

Just before gaining the footbridge and darting under a railway bridge into the foothills on the other side of the road, we will stop for a moment in front of the South Downs Way water tap protruding from the wall. A breather is in order, as a monster climb is uncoiling itself up the track. This is Newmarket Hill, reached by way of another sheer, root-strewn ascent through the trees and giving the impression that it is in no hurry to actually get anywhere any time soon. So we inhale and climb, gingerly at first towards the distant tree line, and then with ecstatic optimism as we turn the corner and make for the gatepost marking the end of purgatory.

In so doing, we have avoided one of the most brutal gradients in the South Downs Way. If we allow our eye to travel down into the turquoise lea, lingering for a moment perhaps on Ashcombe Windmill motionlessly standing guard over Kingston, we will just be able to make it out. A favourite station of the cross for the Jog Shop runners, Kingston Ridge is the bostal to beat them all. Pity the sheep who first set hoof on this path in all innocence of what was being asked of them. But hate them too, because their success created similar expectations of their biped masters. Cut with savage single-mindedness into the hillside, the path offers next to no relief, rearing up with a final vengeance as the longed for plateau comes into view.

But that is no concern of ours today. With Newmarket Hill in the bag, the Moyleman route shuns the path over the ridge to duck down into Castle Hill Nature Reserve. For the most part, this is a charming descent between steep-sided heather-clad slopes, one of which we skirt until we reach the noiseless bowl known to the local running fraternity as Death Valley. Beyond the tumbledown shell of an abandoned farmhouse rises a sinuous hill called the Snake, where the ashes of Chris Moyle himself were scattered. Today, however, we double back on ourselves, bowling through fields of waist-high grass to a beetling track that brings us back up out of the valley onto the South Downs Way.

We are soon on the Yellow Brick Road, startlingly well-paved after our uneven excursions thus far, and set fair for Breaky Bottom Farm a mile or so away over rolling fields. First Kingston, then Swanborough, and finally Rodmell fall away below, as the incinerator at Newhaven grows closer up ahead. Coming off the path, we rush helter skelter down onto Cricketing Bottom farm track, next to which a particularly bulbous crop of pumpkins grows each year. Darting across the much-maligned C7 at the end of the track, we find ourselves at Southease and the unofficial halfway point of the marathon.

Looking down on the abandoned farmhouses in Death Valley from the Snake.

One small step for a marathon runner, one giant leap for his half-marathon running cousin. Leaving one of the county's four round church towers and its achingly attractive green behind, we quicken our step over the Ouse, risking a glance over our left shoulder at the moss-sprinkled cliffs on the edge of Lewes that a select few will tread later in the day. Across the railway track lies Itford Hill, the winding colossus from which it is an easy two-mile lollop to Firle Beacon.

By now, you may have smelled a rat. A humble half-marathon would have stopped in Southease, affording us all the leisure in the world to gaze out over the low-lying brooks that were the last thing Virginia Woolf ever saw before she drowned herself in the Ouse. If we were very still, we might even have seen a little egret, the dazzlingly white wading bird which has lent its name to the (at time of writing) half-finished cycle path between Lewes and Newhaven.

The truth is that this would have been no place to down tools. From the top of Itford we can take stock of all we have achieved since setting out from Lewes at daybreak. Grasp this opportunity because, as soon as we turn our back, our compass points will change. The sight of Mount Caburn, the last heave of the full marathon, will inspire the more ambitious among us with great thoughts, no sooner had than bashfully concealed.

That buzz of static in the air over Firle Beacon car park will have nothing to do with the electricity pylon on the neighbouring rise. Hindsight instead reveals it to be the tingle of possibility.

BARMY ARMY

The Lewes Twitten Run

The idea of running up and down all twelve (and a half) of the twittens on the south side of Lewes High Street first thing on a Sunday morning warrants inclusion in this book on account of its ostensibly barmy genius. The brainchild of Moyleman masterminds Ash Head, Duncan Rawson and Rob Read, it eloquently sums up the glorious futility of hill running – or any running at all, for that matter.

It's easy to forget that Lewes is a hill-fort town situated on a spur of the Downs, with a steep eastern descent via School Hill. The prehistoric valley bottom is bisected by the River Ouse, on the other side of which the land soon rises again to eventually form Mount Caburn. The modern-day twittens, then, describe nothing other than the southern flank of a range of hills that would once have stood in naked splendour over the watery plain now known as Lewes Brooks.

Armed with this historical perspective, you might even consider it the most natural thing in the world to seek out Church Twitten at 9am on the Sabbath and put your best foot forward. In between beginning and ending at the gates of the All Saints Centre, you will emerge blinking onto the High Street exactly twelve times before plunging back down into the twilight zone at the next available opportunity. The whole exercise is compulsive, Sisyphean, potentially hazardous – and a total three-mile blast.

The foot of Keere Street, down whose cobbled incline the Prince Regent famously rode his horse-drawn carriage, is the halfway point. After an obligatory photo, it's back up the hill you've just come down to do it all in reverse. By now, you will have been initiated into the unorthodox ways of the Twitten runner by leading the pack up Green Lane during the first leg of the journey. One descent and another ascent later, you tick off that half-twitten, revealed as the cut-through to the High Street round the back of the Brewers Arms on Stewards Inn Lane.

For an institution that didn't inscribe itself into the local running calendar until autumn 2015, the so-called 'mediæval stairmaster' has a keen sense of its own history. Quite properly, there is a record-holder for the fastest up Keere Street, a duathlon option taking in a post-run dip in the Pell's Pool and an oral archive of extreme variations on the original theme. Over one momentous 24-hour period, Rob ran 26.2 miles-worth of twittens in a uniquely daft take on the Marathon In A Day charity venture.

Runners are creatures of habit – and these are quite religious about the Ground Coffee House at the foot of St Nicholas Lane in which the run ends. For his part, the marathon-running proprietor is a vigorous defender of the steaming runner's right to a refreshment. The perfect blend, if you'll pardon the pun.

Where the twitten runners slake their thirst.

Above: View from Landport Bottom towards Lewes.

Below: Hamsey Church across the water meadows.

Where the axe fell

Lewes – Hamsey – Mount Harry – Lewes
6 miles

One for those yet to be totally won over to the joys of hill running, this route combines gentle stretches along the flat with a testing climb to whet your appetite.

Happily for the purposes of persuasion, the beauty of the initial flat section between Lewes and Hamsey lies to a great extent in the views of the Downs to the left. Starting at Wiley's Bridge, in the corner of Malling Fields behind Tesco, a footpath burrows away along the river bank in the direction of the Landport estate. Tread carefully after rainfall.

Almost straight after the start, Old Malling Church can be seen poking out of the trees on the opposite bank. It has enjoyed an autumn of quiet repose since Dr Beeching's axe fell on the adjacent Uckfield line in the Sixties, reducing the Lewes portion of it to a disused bridge reached by way of a grassy slope whose shape betrays its former life as a railway track. At the end of the path under the bridge, walkers can admire Hamsey Church from a respectful distance.

Back on the other side of the river, we have reached a spot popular with swans and herons. The river briefly widens here, and the occupants of the generous houses on the facing bank have taken advantage of the situation to lash together a private jetty. The rural runner may look forward to escaping the trappings of urban life but the advantage this river path has over the one to Southease and beyond is, in fact, its immunity from the feeling of mud-spattered desolation liable to steal over you somewhere between Iford and Rodmell.

Our chosen peak, Mount Harry, rears up across the brooks to our left. The bright white gash over the Chalk Pit Inn on the Offham road is visible from Firle Beacon on a clear day, but it's particularly impressive up close, as we are soon to find out. Instead of turning right into the village itself once we reach Hamsey, we swing left along Ivors Lane, finally emerging on the other side of the railway track by Offham Church and opposite the Blacksmith's Arms.

The honeymoon period is over. A few strides up the busy main road in the direction of Lewes, an opening in the hedgerow leads to two steep paths up the hill side. The left-hand one breaks the tree line in the form of a series of plateaux anticipating the old quarry a little way along the ridge. The other climbs sharply up the northern flank of Mount Harry. Without the sweeping views of its more precipitous rival, this track nonetheless commands one of the most appealing views of all the hills around Lewes. An irresistible patchwork of cultivated farmland and untamed slopes, stitched together by pylons, takes our mind off the difficulty of our enterprise.

Hovering for a moment on the fringe of the dappled woodland at the top, we have a choice between turning right towards Black Cap or heading back to Lewes via Landport Bottom. Having elected to follow the left-hand path to the quarry, we are soon skimming the rim of the chalk pit on our left before emerging on the north-west edge of the Nevill estate. By following the line of the Old Racecourse road, we then gain the top path shadowing the racecourse itself and begin our gradual descent back down into the town.

A barking man

Lewes – Castle Hill – Woodingdean – Lewes
12 miles

Behind the Swan pub on the Kingston road, a path scuttles up the hillside to emerge on a high bridge spanning the A27.

At the end of the bridge, from which Firle Beacon is clearly visible on the horizon to the south-east, the road hurries on up the chalk embankment. The top is equestrian country, where passers-by are as likely as not to be controlling a skittish horse. To the right of the narrow track to which we have sworn allegiance, a slope falls away towards the dual carriageway.

In the bowl of Castle Hill.

Our faith is rewarded beyond the gate at the end of the path. Here, the undulating field soon straightens out to provide an overwhelming view of Ashcombe Windmill framed against the great bony whaleback of Kingston Ridge. Over our right shoulder, we can see Lewes racecourse; over our left, the golf course inks itself against the sky high on Chapel Hill.

Over the brow of the hill, meanwhile, the path drops down to a fast road through Kingston village. On the other side, a residential lane studded with speed bumps leads to the base of the Downs. At the end of the lane, resist the urge to dart left or right, out of range of the Ridge, and press on to the gate twenty yards shy of the fork in the path.

We are taking the right-hand path today. Granted, it isn't as unforgivingly long as Itford Hill six miles further on, but it's every bit as steep. There's a reason the organisers of the infamous Jog Shop 20 race dwell on Kingston Ridge: it is, to murder a phrase, so sheer they run it twice. What's more, the effect is more pronounced on the right-hand path. At the end of three agonising minutes of ascent, the Amex stadium stands out in the valley far away to the right – for now.

There is no shame in stopping at the top. Indeed, it can be such a lonely spot that any sudden movements are liable to startle walkers. I once succeeded in making a man bark with shock by boldly commenting on the view – so jelly-legged was I after the climb that he hadn't heard me creeping up behind him.

Through a gate on the right and past some scrub, the land climbs again, gently this time. A hard-earned downhill canter later, we're almost at our destination. Keep straight ahead until a sign on the left announces Castle Hill nature reserve. Then leave the Way and descend the chalk path between the heather until you find yourself surrounded by a pallet of colour. Like the secluded dip near Stanmer Park, this is a happily enclosed landscape free of any intimation of traffic.

Another gate under our belts, we follow the line of the field round the imposing hillside, pondering awestruck the gravity-defying antics of the sheep clinging to the opposite flank. Round the bend, the track makes head-on for the derelict farmhouse in Death Valley, the rusty accoutrements of which are scattered around the yard as if set down only yesterday.

The Snake, a hill tortuous and torturous in equal measure, uncoils towards Woodingdean at the end of the farm track. Disturbing the sheep whose habit it is to occupy the shade at the bend in the path, we forge on up the grass slope. It soon earns its name, with a succession of deceiving twists and turns delaying the arrival of the gatepost for what comes to feel an unnecessarily long time. From here, though, the gentlest of climbs soon lifts us clear of the nature reserve and onto high ground overlooking Woodingdean and the seafront far beyond.

Following a rutted chalk track behind a row of houses, our route then passes the first of two pylons that squat on the ridge above the Falmer road. After a swift canter down to the car park metres from the traffic, a hairpin right turn brings us at length up to the second pylon and back to our downland refuge. Kingston Bostal is an undulating mile and a half away as the crow flies.

Before you tumble down the last incline into the village and retrace your footsteps to Lewes, slow down to look out over the Ouse Valley.

Whatever you do, never take that view for granted.

Above: Woodland path to Stanmer Park.

Below: Stanmer church.

A schoolboy's hand

Lewes – Stanmer Park – Lewes
14 miles

I once set off up Spital Lane for Stanmer as a riot broke out in the prison hard by. It also happened to be a day of ominously high winds which caught and dispersed the inmates' cries into a convincing impression of a singing telephone wire. Meanwhile, dust from forest fires on the Iberian peninsula had painted the sky over Lewes an angry shade of red, as if daring me to go ahead with my plan.

At the end of the road, a rough impression in the chalk hillside on our right brings us up to a small paddock. A narrow passageway skirting the compound subsequently leads to a rocky bridle path on the south-west corner of the Nevill estate. From the top of the track, the gaze is inexorably drawn out to sea by the gently insistent line of the Downs inland of Newhaven. The Channel's glare can't quite blot out the slender outline of Ashcombe Windmill above Kingston, though it was lost in shadow on the day of the dust.

As we enter Landport Bottom, a glance to the right yields a different kind of view. The manmade pile of Lewes, with the castle standing proud on the hill, gives way to the Ouse floodplain to the immediate north of the town. A little farther off, modest Hamsey rises timidly out of the meadows like a schoolboy's hand perpetually frozen in mid-air. Even allowing for a greater covering of trees in those days, it's little wonder Simon de Montfort's troops were able to pick off King Henry's men when they got it into their heads to storm Mount Harry before the Battle of Lewes in 1264. They would have quite literally seen them coming a mile off.

With Lewes racecourse running happily wild on our left, we head for the hills. To get to them, we have to pass Jill's Pond at a bend in the field before crossing Old Racecourse Road at the end of the field. Another gate in the top left-hand corner of the next field opens at length onto a chalk track. Black Cap awaits.

Black Cap itself is the ideal distance for a gentle run at the beginning or end of a training cycle. The six-mile round trek from Lewes is just long enough to satisfy you, the hill in which the outward journey culminates just exacting enough to prepare you for more onerous challenges to come. Stanmer is one such challenge.

Beyond the trig point, the ground falls away slightly to the gate onto the South Downs Way. Instead of taking the Housedean Farm turn-off, we forge straight up the track. All about us lies Plumpton Plain, exposed and unkempt on one side and assiduously worked on the other. The Way is our companion until the plateau of Streat Hill moves to intercept us. Just before this meeting of the ways, we pass through a gate on the lefthand side and follow a scarcely discernible trail only separated by a fence from Streat Hill Farm.

Over a stile opposite the last of the outhouses, we find ourselves in open country at last. Left to its own devices, the land rolls luxuriously away towards Stanmer, finally dropping into the valley bottom by way of a narrow track skirting the brow of a vast grassy bowl. Down here, you could be almost anywhere.

The final climb of this leg of the trip is one of the highlights. A sun-dappled path wanders up under the canopy, serenaded by bird song and the rustle of unseen creatures in the undergrowth. But on the final bend a shaft of sunlight shatters the peace. In the clearing at the top, paths disappear into the woods on either side and an electricity pylon looms menacingly in the bushes.

All that remains is to scud down the perilously uneven track into Stanmer village. After a breather at the immaculate church at the end of the main street, you may even be inclined to retrace your steps all the way back to Lewes. Hurry now, the wind's getting up again.

Helter skelter

Falmer – Wolstonbury Hill – Falmer
14 miles

In common with a smattering of high points along the South Downs ridge, Wolstonbury Hill bears all the hallmarks of an Iron Age fort. Looming large over Danny House, the stately pile near Hurstpierpoint where the armistice was signed in 1918, this balding hump is pitted with bunkers instantly revelatory of rudimentary fortifications beneath.

The effect of these ancient ramparts is to obscure the immediate view, cocooning its conquerors in a warped grass bowl that nonetheless offers no arboreal windbreak. Fortunately for the ancients, the spot is uniquely situated for the purposes of long-distance surveillance. Only separated from the western end of the Ditchling Beacon range by a tough climb up Mill Lane to the Jack and Jill Windmills over Clayton, Wolstonbury boasts a raking view along the ridge as far as Chanctonbury Ring and beyond. Newtimber Hill keeps it honest over its shoulder to the south-west.

The view from Wolstonbury, with Jack & Jill windmills top left.

Owing to its position a couple of miles over the West Sussex border, a return trip from Lewes to Wolstonbury is out of reach for all but the real warhorses. For the more masochistic half-marathoners, though, Falmer is a worthy point of departure.

An inconspicuous country lane running round the back of the University of Sussex brings you at length up onto the South Downs Way. After a shady descent under a canopy of trees, a grass-fringed chalk path rises steadily from a farmstead where the road runs out. If you follow the straight unmarked path through open country at the top, Streat Hill Farm soon hoves into view on the left. The Way is at the other end of the adjacent field. Turn left onto it.

No other detours will be necessary until we meet Jack and Jill. The undulating expanses either side of Ditchling Beacon are especially popular with jovial dog-walkers and triumphant cyclists, making this a life-affirming run for reasons that go beyond endorphins and ravishing views. In between cheery greetings, you are at liberty to take in the gunmetal-grey towers arrayed along Brighton seafront, mirrored in the mist by the turbines of Rampion Wind Farm eight miles out to sea.

The Chattri, raised in memory of World War I Indian soldiers.

Once you have put the car park on the summit behind you, you are moving through a landscape that metamorphoses at will between the demon scrub, scorned by naturalists for smothering the carpets of wildflowers with which the Downs has long been associated, and tenacious strips of the rampion (otherwise known as the Pride of Sussex) that have resisted the creep of the thorns. Incidentally, the Castle Hill nature reserve between Kingston and Woodingdean makes a virtue of these prickly interlopers.

A little way down the chalk track leading to Jack and Jill is a fingerpost pointing the way to the Chattri memorial, raised in memory of the Indian soldiers who died of their wounds in Brighton during the First World War. Some 53 Hindu and Sikh warriors were cremated on the spot now occupied by the white marble dome, before having their ashes scattered in the English Channel. The peaceful site adorns an exposed hillside just off the Sussex Border Path and a mile-and-a-half due south of the Way.

On this occasion, however, it is to Wolstonbury that we bend our tracks. Helter skelter down Mill Lane we go, for once spurning the view from the windmill carpark in favour of a cautious skitter along the main road at the foot of the hill. About a hundred yards along the road towards Pyecombe there is a paddock, bordered by a bridleway back up onto the Downs on the other side of the road. This we take; a short climb brings us to a row of gates, of which we choose the one furthest to the right. (For a less hairy route across the A273, see *The Devil of a run* on page 39.)

The upper reaches of Wolstonbury Hill rise out of a beech copse to form a lonely outcrop dressed with a single windswept tree. From the summit, which you reach by way of a gently rising path between high fields on one side and the rim of a coombe on another, the eye falls on a familiar downland feature – one of Kipling's resourceful dew ponds. I advise bringing your own water supply.

RUNNING BLIND

The perils of an excursion by night

It can be fiendishly difficult to combine running with a full-time job.

Some will get up excruciatingly early, racking up the miles before sunrise and returning home for a hard-earned breakfast before work. Others will wait until the working day has drawn to a close, dig out their head torch and toil while their colleagues' thoughts turn to an early night.

Since either option is likely to involve some form of compromise on sleep, neither is particularly appealing to me other than as a last resort. But I subjected myself to the latter one chilly January night, at a time when I felt the scales had tipped excessively in favour of work.

My mistake was to go unequipped. Off-road running by night is a perilous affair at the best of times, as no head torch can illuminate every pothole or shard of flint, but finding your way without any light at all borders on the reckless.

One I bought later . . .

Shortly after gaining the Downs on the edge of Woodingdean, following a well-lit climb from the *Argus* office in Kemp Town, I found out that my mobile phone light just wasn't going to cut it.

From then on, it became an exercise in orienteering. As I hopped gingerly along Kingston Ridge in what I hoped was an easterly direction, I realised I was falling back on stores of muscle memory accumulated on many a diurnal run along the same track. It is striking – if not exactly surprising – just how malign an invisible landscape can feel.

It would not be long, however, until I encountered one of the unexpected thrills of night running: livestock in repose. Framed against the milky glow of distant street lights on the valley floor, a herd of recumbent cattle helpfully traced the edge of the hillside as I stuck doggedly to the top path to Kingston Bostal.

There is nothing like the experience of running blindfold to teach you respect for the wilful rise and fall of a landscape you might otherwise have taken for granted.

The other side of the sword is the happy intimacy such a harum-scarum venture breeds in your relationship with the hillside. If I were given to sermonising, I would tut at urban man's dependence on artificial comforts for peace of mind. Instead, this homily will go no further than pondering the ability of our primitive ancestors to live on the land by the light of nothing more than the sun, the moon and their wits.

I am no zealous convert to night running just yet – unlike the silhouette in its glowing headgear that passed me going the other way at the foot of the bostal that evening – but I offer this break-out for the benefit of those hardy readers for whom hill running in daytime is not enough of an adventure.

Devil's Dyke looking west, with Chanctonbury Ring in the middle distance.

The devil of a run

Lewes – Devil's Dyke – Saddlescombe Farm
15 miles

As double-figure runs to the west of Lewes go, this one must rank among the very toughest.

It's a run that creeps up on you, with a forgiving stretch between Black Cap and the Jack and Jill windmills hardly preparing you for what is to come further along the South Downs Way. The best advice I can give is not to run up and down Mount Caburn twice the day before you do it.

Given the amount of time we've already spent on that section of the trail, I won't bother sketching the route between Lewes Prison and the windmills, save to say that it is a useful vantage point from which to size up the scale of the challenge ahead. To the immediate south-west of Wolstonbury Hill's bald peak looms its near neighbour, Newtimber, willing us nearer if we dare.

The South Downs Way forks left just up the track from Jack and Jill and takes an idling course down past Pyecombe golf club before meeting the A273. Having opened with an exaggeratedly expansive gesture of welcome just moments earlier, the countryside goes into hiding at this juncture as the path takes another left turn on the other side of the road – don't turn right, or you'll end up on the Wolstonbury track – and scurries off into the winning village of Pyecombe.

The quietly beautiful village church compels you to stop and stare for a moment, which is just as well as the toughest climb of the day is a matter of minutes away. With an almost palpable grimace of distaste, the Way rushes downhill and crosses a road bridge over the A23, before turning left down a wide track and hugging an industrial estate – attached to Wayfield Park farm – for a couple of hundred yards. Buried in the perimeter fence just before the dual carriageway bends towards Brighton, a merciful path bears you up and out of the chaos past an attractive farm cottage.

But you would do well to handle this path with care, for it does not really have your best interests at heart. It may have offered you salvation from possibly the ugliest section of the 100-mile footpath, but it is an almighty slog to the summit, especially if the going is muddy. That's because this is Newtimber Hill. Just when you think you've reached the top, it turns out you haven't.

But it always comes in the end, and the reward is a gentle jog down the other side to Saddlescombe Farm, on the site of a 3,000-year-old settlement. The track passes picturesque cottages on the right before circumventing an assortment of farmyards and barns – currently in National Trust hands – on the left and hitting the Henfield road. On the other side, a steep path leads up to the rim of Devil's Dyke.

This stretch can seem endless to tired limbs, not least because you are painfully aware of the Dyke disappearing in your wing mirrors as the path resolutely refuses to turn. Said to be Satan's work, the plunging valley below turns hikers into diminishing specks before swallowing them entirely. Finally, the gate hoves into view and the reason for your journey unfurls in front of you.

Where the road runs out in front of the Devil's Dyke pub up ahead, West Sussex appears laid out in its entirety. As long as the wind is not so brisk as to bring tears to your eyes, you will be able to see all the way to Chanctonbury Ring and beyond. From up there, no onlooker can do other than marvel at the way the smooth humps of the Downs play a never ending game of tag with the light, each one always one step ahead of its pursuer. In my biased opinion, this sight is balm to any aches and pains accumulated over thirteen-plus miles of undulating countryside.

You could stop here and dive into the pub, but then you would be missing out on a detour through Poynings. After picking your way back down into the valley on the other side of the pub, via a mixture of open woodland and exposed hillside, you emerge at length onto the village's main thoroughfare and pass the Royal Oak pub before entering a field just before a bend in the road.

From here, it's a pleasant ramble back to the farm – well, almost. Over the first stile on your left, round a pond and along a winding woodland path you go, until the Dyke fills your field of vision again. At this point, you have no choice but to climb off the valley floor by way of a wide grassy ridge that snakes languidly to a gate halfway up the hillside. Crest the brow of the rise beyond, and you are the length of an unkempt field away from the safe haven of Saddlescombe.

Just don't forget to arrange a lift.

The pond at Saddlescombe Farm.

Above: The view east from Ditchling Beacon.

Below: The National Trust and the Sussex Wildlife Trust manage separate areas of the Beacon.

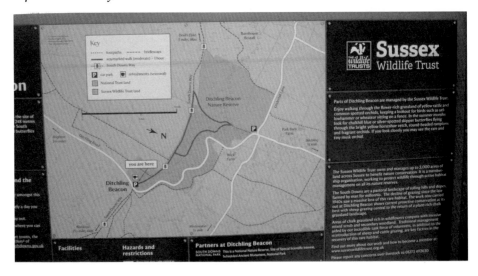

Definitely not easy

'13 The Hard Way' half marathon
Clayton – Housedean Farm – Clayton
13.1 miles

On ill thought-out trail runs in Germany I first encountered the ominous expression 'kein betreutes Wohnen'. Though I've never settled on a satisfactory translation for a phrase that literally means 'unsupervised living', it kept on going round and round my head as I tackled the 13 The Hard Way half marathon for the first time in the high summer of 2017.

Then a year old, the course would live up to its name. It begins, in typically unglamorous fashion, in a field off Underhill Lane, a narrow road snaking along the bottom of Ditchling Beacon from Westmeston to Clayton. After emerging opposite the Lodge Lane junction and turning left, runners are almost immediately brought up short by a vicious track up the spur, known locally as the Tank Tracks after its inadvertent excavation by manoeuvring Canadian troops during the Second World War.

Do not be fooled by the shady stretch at the beginning of the ascent: this is sheer, exposed and, as the Sussex Trail Events organisers insouciantly inform you beforehand, steeper the higher you climb. Those with one eye on the view will appreciate the lightly wooded escarpment rushing down towards Clayton on the right and the generous cushion provided by the tufty foothills to the left. Those blind to all but their time will simply focus on not stopping. Given that the path is by now strewn with contestants slowing to a grim walk, the latter is no mean feat.

At the top, your reward is an easy lollop over the fields to Ditchling Beacon. For a mile or more, the terrain is forgivingly undulating, brushing riotously colourful wildflowers on the left and expansive farmland falling away towards the coast on the right.

A water stop in the car park at the summit equips you for the rough and tumble of the next mile, mitigated by the sight of the Amex stadium at Falmer and the toyset tiles of Westmeston.

Much of the initial overtaking will be out of the way by the time you scud down the cattle track onto the chalk path near Streat Hill Farm. The farm traffic allowing, a jagged path soon brings you out onto Plumpton Plain, at which point the right-hand Housedean turn is close. Haunted by memories of a cramped recent trot along the top path between two beetling tractors, I made sure to open up a meaningful gap between myself and my nearest challenger before the turn-off. A tangle of limbs on the narrow ridge over Housedean is the last thing you want, as I was reminded later.

It's also a crying shame to be distracted from the unfurling vista on your left. If you look back the way you came, you can glimpse the trig point on Black Cap. Then let your eye wander luxuriantly down to Ashcombe Windmill and up to Kingston Ridge, streaking away to South Farm at one end and Woodingdean at the other. Strain your eyes and you will even be able to make out the white chalkpit cliffs overlooking the River Ouse outside Lewes. If you are lucky, the peregrine falcon pair that once nested in a mossy alcove on the cliff-face may even be sentimentally riding the thermals above their long-gone shelter.

Now release the handbrake. I made my most significant gains on the downward slope into Housedean, reeling in the stragglers of the chasing pack in time to go toe to toe with them up Heart Attack Hill and blinking into the sunlight over the A27. One scarcely controlled descent to the halfway point later and I was confronted with a heaving table of banana bread, jelly babies and nectarines. More efficient bodies than mine might be able to stomach cake halfway through a thirteen-mile bog trot; I had a solitary jelly bean, took a fistful for the journey and then tossed them into the bushes after catching my quarry once and for all on the way back up the incline.

Retracing your steps back up to the South Downs Way six and a half miles into 13 The Hard Way may provide hard evidence of the futility of competitive long-distance running. But it can also be a morale boost to see dozens coming the other way, each and every one contributing to a surreal downland manoeuvre decked out in synthetic technicolour. This section of the course also happens to be the one that makes or breaks the ambitious runner. Either you slow to an agreeable jog and let the gangly frontrunners push ahead, or you grit your teeth and step into their slipstream. Your decision could well make the difference between a finishing time of two hours plus or the fabled 'sub-two'.

I chose the latter. Finding myself in an earnest knot of runners returning along the perilously slender track I had hurried onto half an hour earlier, I then had to make a pragmatic call. Any runner will be familiar with the dilemma of simply sustaining their pace, thereby staying in the comfort zone, or putting a chink of daylight between themselves and their companions. My own quandary was made more pressing by the utterly prosaic difficulty of remaining

Jack and Jill windmills above Clayton.

upright in a throng moving at speed through a confined space. So I blinked first, breaking away along the plateau and leading our band of brothers up and out of Housedean to rejoin the chalk path back to Ditchling Beacon.

Then a strange sight. A tall man in his late sixties, who had ignored me on the way out, still stood on the edge of the fields half a mile distant, a water bottle in his limply extended hand. Such was his deflated demeanour that he might have been mistaken for a hitch-hiker if he hadn't been the one offering charity. When I passed him, I had just been overtaken for the last time and was disinclined to give another inch to my pursuers. However, his presence had succeeded in confirming the matter-of-fact generosity feats of even moderate athleticism inspire in the general public.

Back over the Beacon we go on this most simple of all there-and-back trips. After stretching your legs down some of the earlier ups, you can begin ticking off the checkpoints between you and the final juddering dash down the Tank Tracks. Conventional wisdom has it that you should 'let your legs go' on the downhills, hesitant descents actually exerting more of a strain on already tense knee joints. I duly flew down the hill, doing my best to ignore the impact while sending up silent prayers to the gods who watch over our tendons.

Hard? Yes. Worth every minute? You guessed it.

The sun in your eyes

Round Hill Romp 10k race
Steyning – Chanctonbury Ring – Steyning
10km/6.2 miles

Leaving Steyning's fetching High Street, with its striking clock tower and timbered inn, a narrow lane leads off into the skirts of the Downs. A couple of miles distant, the northern face of Chanctonbury Ring looms large.

On an airless summer's evening, this route poses two problems that have little to do with running and everything to do with the gradually setting sun. Over the course of a mile under the canopy, the eyes laboriously adjust to the gloaming, only for a blinding glare to scatter the shadows as you emerge onto an extension of Mouse Lane bisecting classically quilted Sussex farmland. Through the haze at the end of the track, you can just about make out Wiston House, from the site of which the land on either side has been administered since the Saxons.

Chanctonbury Ring from Mouse Lane.

Today, the manor is an occasional base for Foreign and Commonwealth Office conferences. It was back in 1760, though, that Charles Goring, the great-great-grandfather of the current landowner, changed the face of 'Chankburry' forever by planting a ring of beech trees on the summit of the hill that had watched over his childhood. The 1989 hurricane that still gives blundering weatherman Michael Fish sleepless nights destroyed three-quarters of the copse, before it was faithfully regrown by bereft downlanders.

This is our destination. To begin the beetling, root-strewn ascent, you turn off Mouse Lane and duck down onto a shady pass flanked by high hedgerows. If you hadn't already realised you were in the foothills, the sudden encroachment of trees around your head soon sets you right. At the sight of the first tussock, some runners instantly flop into a walk.

A steady climb through cool woodland offers a near unbroken view of the Weald unfurling from the base of the down. The Ring itself is seen in profile, the racing green of its foliage offset by the softer emerald of the escarpment. From the bostal, you would be well placed to see the Devil appear, if an anti-clockwise circuit of the Ring repeated seven times really were to give the folk tale credence by calling forth Beelzebub on the slopes of Chanctonbury Hill.

For now, however, you have a job to do. This is uneven chalk downland at its most energy-sapping, one of those paths that looks as if it came about entirely by accident, and the gradient is the only constant. Ragged breathing is interrupted only by yelps of protest and the occasional vituperative outburst seemingly directed at some dimly-imagined pagan god held responsible for making these hills.

When the fifth corner gives way to yet another a further fifty yards ahead, the time has come to dig in. But this vertical tunnel up above Steyning is a pure insight into the psychology of the runner. As your legs turn to lead and the longed-for brow of the hill holds itself tantalisingly out of reach, all you have left is the belief that it will end. That, and little else, is what is going through the mind of each and every one of the people toiling up that inexorably rising slope.

Then you are out, blinking, into the sunshine. Your reward for a mile-long climb is a view of the glittering Channel, framed by the sweeping border of the Downs falling away towards Worthing. Running with your back to the Ring, you watch the hills play cat-and-mouse with themselves, doubling back on themselves with a familiar, languid shrug that holds you spellbound.

The track then briefly joins up with our old friend, the South Downs Way, before edging round the hill via a narrow, thorny path that drops precipitously at intervals. For a mile, you are under the trees again, squinting through the artificial dusk for rabbit holes. The trail bobs and weaves to the five mile mark, then it's downhill all the way.

Scudding downhill into the range of the loud hailer down on the cricket green, the runner has a dilemma. The trees are about to clear to reveal the Weald in all its pillowy glory below, and any racer with regard for their knees, let alone their time, would be well advised to 'let go' at that point. The most seasoned competitors will exploit this stretch to overtake at the first hint of hesitation, whereupon momentum is likely to carry them all the way round the last corner, onto the home straight and across the finish line. If you trust the hills to catch you as you fall, though, you stand a chance of holding off the charge of the flight brigade.

This is an unusually taxing 10k course, so you owe it to yourself to take in the view from the finish line. If it weren't for the shape of a straggler moving through the fading light high up, it could almost pass for a painting.

I can't forget the lane that goes from Steyning to the Ring
In summer time, and on the downs how larks and linnets sing
High in the sun. The wind comes off the sea, and, oh, the air!
I never knew till now that life in old days was so fair.
But now I know it in this filthy rat-infested ditch,
Where every shell must kill or spare, and God alone knows which.
And I am made a beast of prey, and this trench is my lair;
My God, I never knew till now that those days were so fair.
And we assault in half-an-hour, and it's a silly thing:
I can't forget the lane that goes from Steyning to the Ring

Written by John Stanley Purvis (using the name Philip Johnson)
5th Battalion, Yorkshire Regiment, on 2nd December 1915, in a
trench behind the Somme. The original stone was placed in the
lane by the people of Steyning in 2000 AD in celebration of their
inheritance, and replaced, after damage to the original, in 2006 AD.

Above: The plaque with John Stanley Purvis's poem in praise of the road to Chanctonbury Ring.

Below: Looking down on the Wildbrooks from Amberley Mount.

Above the Wildbrooks

Steyning – Amberley
12 miles

There is more obviously lovely countryside along the South Downs Way than that between the winning villages of Steyning and Amberley – not least because the A24 slices straight through it, compelling the runner to dodge across the dual carriageway at the halfway stage.

But it is a route that amply repays your patience, for it begins in the high wooded splendour of Chanctonbury and ends in the moist flatlands of the Arun Valley, a feat of teleportation possible only in hilly country. Do not be fooled by the Downs' unhurried course: it can disguise grand set changes on the plain below.

Our journey begins on Mouse Lane, which leads off Steyning High Street at a bend in the road. This understated little road is, in fact, the subject of a poem by Yorkshire clergyman John Stanley Purvis, written just before he went over the top in one of the Great War's many unnamed acts of bloodletting and shown on the facing page. A touching articulation of overpowering nostalgia when all seems lost, the words are etched into a stone several hundred yards along the lane on the right.

Opposite this tablet, a rough footpath on the other side of a gate rises gradually, then abruptly, to the treeline half a mile above your head. The going is slippery after snowfall, but it is steep whatever the weather. Anti-climax is your instant reward at the top, with the brow of the hill stubbornly refusing to give way until you have followed a narrow path to the right as far as it goes and then turned left towards the sea and onto the South Downs Way.

I defy anyone not to be unsettled by Chanctonbury Ring, which stands starkly on the hill a mile further along the ridge. Myths abound – one mentioned in the previous chapter – investing the circle of trees with a satanic significance that has withstood its partial ruin during the Great Storm of 1987. On the approach to the Ring, it is hard to escape the feeling that you are stepping into its baleful sphere of influence.

So it is with a sigh of relief that we turn our backs on the copse and carry on along the Way, passing a dew pond on our right. Soon enough the path turns briskly to the right and swoops down to the A24 west of Washington. On the other side of the dual carriageway a road climbs away to the right and emerges on a path running through open fields past a run-down farm outhouse.

No dramatic escarpments will command the eye for the next couple of miles until a lonely bouquet of sign posts points the way to Storrington, Long Furlong and Amberley. A couple of miles to the west a narrow line of trees marches across the horizon and down into the valley. In the time it takes us to reach it, the path will have stolen closer to the ridge and a glimpse of dusky blue hundreds of feet below.

At the top of the slope, beyond Kithurst Hill car park, a treat awaits. Almost as far as the eye can see, the River Arun snakes away across the vast shimmering floodplain that is Amberley Wildbrooks. Its many arteries disperse themselves across a happily waterlogged landscape serenaded by composer John Ireland in a solo piano piece named after the wetlands that so captured his imagination. This is the scene, unmatched on the drier plains of East Sussex, which launched a thousand chords.

The path loses its vantage point as it tumbles down Amberley Mount to the prosaically named Downs Farm. From here, the track descends swiftly past a sloping field of tottering lambs, before emptying out onto the road into the village.

Where royals misbehaved

Uppark – West Harting Down – Harting Down – Uppark
10 miles

At a bend in the road leading to Uppark, ancestral pile of the Fetherstonhaughs and home to an infant H.G. Wells, a path snakes away left and right. This inconspicuous track is, in fact, the home straight of the Sussex section of the South Downs Way.

Follow it west past a field of purple petals, and you will be in Hampshire in a matter of minutes. The Sussex Border Path is a fairly recent invention, which may account for the absence of a sign at the fork in the road by an apparently derelict barn where it intersects with the Way. Fortunately, the continuation of the latter path is clearly marked.

A gentle rise in the chalk trail brings you out onto a ridge, from which an improbably bucolic scene presents itself for your inspection. In so complementary a fashion do the farmhouses array themselves on either side of the declining road ahead that you

A view of the copper spire of South Harting church.

would not be overly surprised to see Bilbo Baggins totter out of one, wreathed in allegorical pipe smoke.

The hikers you have been passing for the last ten minutes will push on towards Winchester, a mere marathon distance away at the end of a 100-mile trek. Eyes narrowed in pursuit of their goal, they will hardly notice the bridlepath on their left climbing steadily up into the characteristic woodland of West Harting Down. Hemmed in by thick belts of trees on the county border, this sun-dappled stretch lends itself to meditations on the whims of cartographers and the liminal places they unwittingly usher into being.

I called the woodland on these slopes characteristic because it immediately distinguishes a West Sussex hillside from any of its

Beacon Hill looking towards Butser Hill at the westernmost end of the South Downs Way.

eastern counterparts. Whereas the Downs between Wolstonbury Hill and Beachy Head are remarkable for the scarcity of vegetation on their flanks, trusting instead to their sweeping vistas to impress, those from Newtimber all the way to Butser flaunt their natural covering to striking effect.

At precisely the point at which contemplative calm begins to give way to claustrophobia back on the bridlepath, a track doubling back under the trees invites you to scorn both the paths in front of you in favour of that fleeting acquaintance, the Sussex Border Path. This takes you to the fringe of the woods, and thither to the South Downs Way crossroads.

A glance to port reveals the recently vacated down in all its wooded splendour, bedecked on the day I passed through in an autumnal pallet that was a joy to behold. The view to starboard, meanwhile, is drawn magnetically to the Vandalian Tower, stranded on high in a remote corner of the Uppark estate on the other side of the main road.

That ruined folly, the site of many a drunken revelry in the days when Uppark was frequented by badly-behaved royalty and Nelson's mistress Lady Hamilton danced on the dining table in the house, calls like a lapidary siren as you return along the Way to the starting point.

Rejoining the path heading east, you start climbing straight away. The path runs parallel with the road below in a manner reminiscent of Ditchling Bostal almost fifty miles to the east, but it's not as punishing. Across the road at the top, ravishing views towards the North Downs take in the towering copper spire of South Harting in the foreground, with Butser Hill, the highest point in the entire South Downs range, easily distinguishable to the west.

From the valley floor a mile further east along the ridge, there rears a sheer peak by the unimaginative name of Beacon Hill. The path is more of a rut, the gradient practically vertical. Pause for a breather at the gate, then crest the brow of the hill for your rendezvous with the trig point.

Up here, you are poised between Sussex and Hampshire, high above a twilight realm of coombes with names like Kill Devil Copse. No seagull ventures up to these heights, though the gleaming Solent at your back is a reminder that the South Downs are never far from the sea.

Eastbourne, according to a fingerpost at the foot of the hill, is 62 miles away. For now, though, Uppark will do.

BODY MANAGEMENT

Injuries are a runner's worst nightmare. Over several months of marathon training, I lived in fear of the slightest niggle – to the point of paranoia, if truth be told.

But the good news is that most setbacks are avoidable, as long as you don't commit the cardinal sin of thinking you are invincible.

Take it from a reformed idiot. Living in Hamburg after graduating, and long before any idea of the Moyleman entered my head, I got into the habit of setting off for pacey dawn slogs around the streets near my flat several times a week. Looking back now on my pre- and post-run routine is enough to make me wince.

That's mainly because there wasn't one. I worked a standard 9–5 job, making each morning outing a race against the clock. Mindful of the time, I would simply pull on my gear, leave the building and run. As if that weren't enough, it was often bitterly cold as well.

When I pulled up with excruciating knee pain towards the end of my four-month stay, it didn't immediately occur to me that I had done anything wrong. Had I turned awkwardly when I rounded that corner between the vegan supermarket and the carvery? Or had I begun to sprint too early? That was as far as the inquest went.

There might have been a grain of truth in the second thought. You should never launch straight into a headlong dash before your muscles are warmed up properly. But then you shouldn't run at all until you have stretched thoroughly. If you think that sounds boring, you would be right. But if you think it sounds neurotic, you are on to a loser before you have even begun.

My German agony should have been the wake-up call I needed. But I failed to properly heed it – it turns out that the occasional 'one leg forward, one leg back' does not cut it if you are trying to up your mileage, especially if you're running on testing terrain like the Downs. Oblivious to the lurking danger, I returned home, recovered at length from the first injury, and then went back to the hills in earnest after an eight-month absence.

The help of a chiropractor had been phase one in Operation Get To Know The Body Of Which You Are Asking So Much. When still struggling with knee pain, I threw myself upon her mercy and discovered that my spine wasn't entirely straight. Believe it or not, there was nothing out of the ordinary in this, but nobody with pretensions to a long running career could have ignored such a revelation in good conscience. So I inserted an insole under the shorter left leg, corrected the curvature and swiftly felt the benefits of having a body that evenly distributed the strain of off-road running, instead of concentrating the impact in one knee joint.

But I wasn't out of the woods yet. Knee trouble returned with a vengeance a month or two after my 13 The Hard Way outing. Mystified and increasingly frustrated, I sought the help of a physiotherapist. She was the first person to impress on me the vital importance of 'managing your body' as a runner. This means stretching on rest days, too, in order to keep your calves and hamstrings supple and to ease the burden on your all too vulnerable knees. It isn't enough simply to react to injuries: you have to pre-empt them, too.

My problem was that I had underestimated the importance of the knee as the hinge between your calf and your thigh. I wasn't stretching either of the last two enough before and after runs, leaving them tight and unable to absorb the strain I was putting them under. The knees had evidently taken the view 'If you want something done, you'd better do it yourself', and now they were paying the price for my recklessness. The improvement in both my condition and the elasticity of my calf muscles was instant. Within a week, I was healed.

But even now, my education was not complete. If you want to run further than you ever have, you need to accept pain as part of the bargain. We may have been born to run, as one celebrated running book bullishly proclaims, but we have lost the knack as a species. Coaxing a convenience-crowded twenty-first century body into meaningful action over many miles of rough country, while preferable to the percussive beat of road-running, is bound to hurt at first. This is where hot baths come in.

I'm a late convert to a scalding soak, but I find its effects so soothing that I've been known to resort to a pre-run bath as a means of heading off any nagging stiffness ahead of a hefty trudge.

Afterwards, it's a non-negotiable must. But don't substitute a bath for a session of stretches. You may balk at the idea of yet more exertion after an unprecedently long run, but it's about being cruel to be kind. Unless you're blessed with self-healing muscle fibres, there is no getting around it.

None of which is to say that stretching is a panacea. But you'll have to read on to find out why.

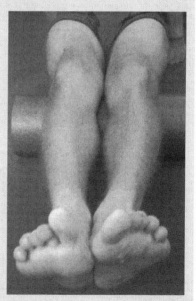

On a roll: post-run sessions with a roller have also helped weary hamstring and calf muscles to hold up in training. The routine, known by scientists as myofascial release, is a form of DIY massage designed to relax over-worked muscle fibres (fasciae).

Dear Moyleman Runner

The Moyleman team have been out today marking the course ready for tomorrow. Unless conditions deteriorate overnight and the forecast becomes worse than expected, we're very pleased to say that it is our judgement that the event will be able to take place.

However, please don't underestimate how demanding the conditions are. The Moyleman team are pretty seasoned runners who know the terrain extremely well. We experienced the conditions on the top of the Downs today as harsh, with strong and very cold northeasterly winds. The windchill effect is forecast to be minus 8 degrees, making running very uncomfortable in the exposed sections that are found all around the course. Moreover, there are parts of the run that are remote from immediate road access, making it slow to get off the course should you need to.

We are therefore strongly recommending to all runners that you wear a hat, gloves, neckwear and have multiple layers of clothing, including a jacket. We would advise that you don't run in shorts. We would also suggest that any solo runners might consider teaming up with others as you go round the course, rather than running wholly on your own.

Remember, just getting round the Moyleman is a challenge in itself. Tomorrow will not be about times, it's about taking care of yourselves and each other.

With kind regards
Duncan (Race Director)

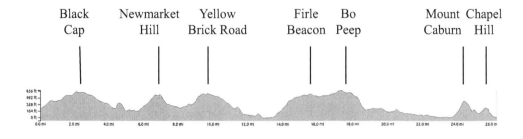

The Moyleman

26.2 miles

I sure know how to pick 'em. An email from the Moyleman team the day before the 2018 race made it ominously clear that my first marathon was going to be by far the hardest in the event's four-year history. A weather front glibly dubbed the Beast from the East had south-east England in its icy grip – and all bets were off.

That included the dread question of whether it would even go ahead. Cancellation was a very real possibility with just 48 hours to go, threatening to throw months of meticulous planning into jeopardy. Light snowfall, coupled with biting winds and plunging temperatures, conspired to keep organisers on the edge of their seats until race day dawned on Sunday, March 18.

All the uncertainty was enough to deter dozens of runners from even turning up, with the 250-plus who did crowding into Wallands School hall in Lewes with a palpable air of trepidation. We had been told in that email to forget personal bests (if we had them) and concentrate on simply getting round the course. The idea of running in pairs had even been floated, lending the whole occasion the touching feel of a school trip – without the temper tantrums.

When race director Duncan yelled 'Go!' and we all began to potter up Landport Bottom, I began to turn over in my mind the achievement of even making it this far. For a while, the fiendish conditions were even forgotten as I motored happily towards the first climb of the day, Black Cap. I had crossed this stretch of countryside so many times over the past two years – but never like this. Today I was going to enter uncharted territory.

After Black Cap the countryside drops down into Housedean Farm, a route I had followed at a brisker pace on a half-marathon the previous summer. The countryside here opens up in front of you like a pastel painting, with Ashcombe Windmill drawing your eye to the south-east. To your left and right are scenes typical of East Sussex, with the sweeping escarpment of Kingston Ridge offsetting the plainer lower reaches of Black Cap, clad in classically scraggly scrub.

After crossing the A27 via a breathless scramble up Heart Attack Hill, runners face the first big climb of the day. Known by some in the local running fraternity as The Relentless Bastard, Newmarket Hill is a reasonably gentle incline but makes up in length what it lacks in gradient. At the top, a right turn soon takes you west along the track to Castle Hill nature reserve. A quarter of an hour later you take a steep farm track back up onto the ridge.

The halfway point at Southease is half an hour's trot away, at the other end of the Yellow Brick Road. Up here, you can make out the incinerator at Newhaven as the land falls away towards the sea. You can also begin to reset your compass as Firle Beacon hoves into view to the left. Mount Caburn, the day's final checkpoint, looms large to the east.

But first you must navigate the dispiritingly long track through South Farm, known as Cricketing Bottom. On the other side of the C7, it's a comfortable canter past Southease's round-towered church and down to the river. Beyond the railway track, a welcome party – in both senses of the word – will be ready and waiting to congratulate the half-marathoners and gee up the lunatics.

By then, I could tell something was wrong. Cramp, which thrives on low temperatures, had first made its presence felt around mile twelve in the form of an unfamiliar yet unmistakeable twinge in my right calf. Applying totally incongruous footballing logic, I decided I would 'run it off'. Never having encountered it before in all my painstaking – and painful – hours of training, I had no reason to suppose it would derail my marathon attempt. After all, I told myself five minutes later, I had made it to halfway inside the top 50 in a field of 250 runners, some of whom had been loping around these heights since I was a schoolboy.

After a quick food break, I began gingerly to scale Itford Hill. This one has a strong claim to be the most agonising climb of the day, with any progress made around the base of the beast sure to be brought up short round the bend in the track. The end never seems to come, with the majority wisely electing to power walk instead of forcing their legs into an ungainly and futile shuffle.

It was at the top of Itford that the clammy hand of cramp began to steal over me once and for all. My discomfort was mingled with a terrible sense of injustice given that I had run a similar route barely a week before without a care in the world. Why today of all days? The answer, of course, lay in the weather. The best laid plans of mice and men gang aft agley, and this particular enactment of the poet's timeless line had ample helpings both of meticulous preparation and imponderable, indifferent misfortune.

Still I soldiered on to Firle Beacon, refusing to contemplate the prospect of failure. This is the point in the race at which thoughts and necks turn towards Caburn, and the finish line emerges through a fog of doubt in the shape of a realistic vision of triumph. The most serene of runners may even notice how the harbour arm at Newhaven briefly appears as a natural extension of the River Ouse, which snakes lazily across the floodplain from Lewes on its unhurried journey to sea. Only the hills seemingly stand in its way.

Beyond the car park, tiring runners can take solace in the fact they are entering the final ten miles of trudge. My own relief was short-lived, as my legs seized up barely half a mile along the ridge to Bo Peep, where the course leaves the Downs for the penultimate time. I had felt strong, comfortable and bound for glory – only to see it all taken away by the indiscriminate hand of fate.

In the half an hour between my first collapse and heartbreaking withdrawal, I knew pain as I had never experienced it. Both legs cramped up all the way down, turning me into a statue no good for standing let alone running. But worse – far worse – than the physical distress were its emotional symptoms.

In that same half an hour of reluctant, tear-stained capitulation, however, I also experienced the very best of humanity: my fellow runners who tried in vain to restore my legs to some kind of feeling as we walked the painful mile to the next marshal point; the passing stranger who donated a salt capsule and his foil sheet in exchange for nothing but my gasped thanks; and the photographer on his way to the hilltop in his car who offered to drive me back to Lewes instead of joining his wife to act as her support runner for the remaining eight miles.

Good Samaritans: two hitherto unknown fellow runners coax me towards the marshal point at Bo Peep. [Photo courtesy James McCauley]

These were the people I was thinking of as the Old Coach Road flashed regrettably by in the wing mirror, dotted with brave and selfless runners mentally gearing themselves up for the ascent of Mount Caburn that lay beyond the end of the rutted track that runs parallel with the A27.

Dear reader, do not be fooled by the pretty little village of Glynde, reached on race day only by way of an underpass beneath the dual carriageway. Here – at the end of the high street past the cricket green, to be precise – there be dragons.

Another time, then . . .

Afterword

The Moyleman solo and the Three Forts Challenge (27.2 miles)

There can be few human impulses more powerful than a sense of unfinished business.

It was about eighteen miles into the Three Forts Challenge – seven weeks after my Moyleman dreams had run aground on bitterly cold temperatures – that I realised this.

By now, I had laid the ghost of my home marathon by tackling the course solo. The stubborn imprint of cramp left over from race day made for a ponderous circuit, but I still descended on an empty Harvey's Yard with a euphoria lost on passers-by and the renewed conviction that my official attempt had been derailed by nothing more than a combination of bad luck and ghastly weather.

Since joining Lewes Athletics Club in the days after that first disappointment, I had also regained an acute appreciation of the simple joy of running without any goals in mind. Marathon training is an all-consuming business, and it is all too easy to forget why you started running in the first place. Becoming a member of Lewes AC brought that carefree, questing thrill flooding back, drawing the sting from the hours spent on solitary training runs in intense pursuit of a particular mileage.

And yet. The desire to complete a competitive downland marathon still nagged away at the back of my mind like an itch that needed to be scratched. Days after the Moyleman, I put my name down for the Three Forts, a notorious trail race that, by dint of being a shade over 27 miles long, technically qualifies as an ultra-marathon. It would be a shame, I reasoned, to waste all that training.

But as May 6 neared, it became clear it was going to be a scorcher. In the week prior to the event, fatigue followed by a sore throat had already conspired to make the idea of switching to the half-marathon option for an extra fiver sorely tempting. I gulped when

I saw the forecast: 20 degrees and cloudless. Up on the exposed stretches of the Downs, you could add a couple of extra degrees to that figure.

It proved a conservative estimate, with temperatures on the day peaking around 25 centigrade and spots of shade all too infrequent. As with the Moyleman, personal bests were off the table. This would be about getting round – and if I spent too long cursing my misfortune in being saddled with extreme conditions for the second time in a matter of weeks, even that would slip from my grasp. Again.

As everyone I spoke to on the way round agreed, just turning up on the start line at Hill Barn Recreation Ground in Worthing was half the battle. Once the race started, there was mercifully little time to contemplate the first climb of the day, with the two-mile ascent to Cissbury Ring upon us before we had the chance to break our stride in preparation. Cissbury, the first of the forts that give the route its name, is one of the many Iron Age strongholds scattered the length and breadth of the South Downs. Over the course of its unfathomably long life, it has been put to use as a Neolithic flint mine, a Roman bulwark against potential Saxon raids and a base for anti-aircraft guns in the Second World War. That mad May day, it would find its true calling as a key way-station for a herd of hill runners.

Not that any but those in the leading pack were in the mood to run many of the hills on this occasion. After Cissbury, the route picks its way along a couple of miles of farm tracks before emerging to the north of Lancing College, distinguished by what's claimed to be the largest school chapel in the world. On the coast, Shoreham power station looms large and oppressive. Then a steep drop to the A283 outside Upper Beeding, by way of a country lane through the village of Botolphs, brings you to the River Adur crossing.

Above: Devil's Dyke, the easternmost point of the Three Forts ultra.

Below: The steep gradients of the Three Forts Challenge have earned it the nickname 'The Tough One'.

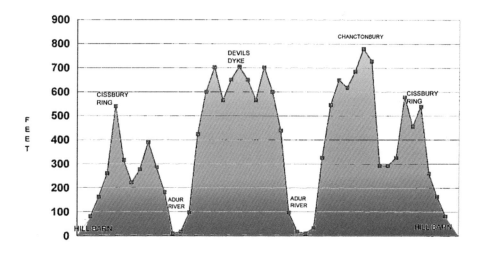

On the other side of the main road, we dropped as one into a grim trudge up Truleigh Hill. As the gradient increased, a man in front of me whipped out a heavy-duty camera and began to talk, as if programmed.

'We're seven miles into the Three Forts Challenge,' he said. 'It's also the 61-mile point of the South Downs Way 100 . . .'

Comedic value had not been entirely absent, with one fellow runner at the four-mile stage correcting an interested observer to the effect that we would be running twenty-seven miles, not twenty-six: 'I couldn't let it lie,' he smiled.

At the top of Truleigh the route flattened out again for three miles, carrying us past the television pylons beneath which a vital wartime radar station was once concealed. With the sun climbing high in the sky by now, we took a ducking-and-diving chalk path that bore us at length up and over the ridge to the easternmost extremity of the run at Devil's Dyke (fort two). Aid stations had been liberally distributed throughout the first half of the route, and the one at this juncture was gratefully received at the end of an eleven-mile slog that felt more like thirteen.

This was also where I began to implement the abiding lesson of the Moyleman. Unsurprisingly, that sun was exacting a heavy toll in sweat, and I had to head off creeping dehydration if I was to stand any chance of getting round the course without doubling up in nutrient-starved cramps for the second time in weeks. I had been sipping water every mile or so over the first ten miles, but I now had a trump card for when the going got tough: electrolyte tablets. On the eve of the race I'd dissolved a couple of these in a bottle of water in the knowledge that at some point I was going to have to replenish my natural stores. That time was now.

For the next four miles – with the exception of a passing twinge just after halfway – taking repeated sips of the stuff, coupled with an energy bar, worked tolerably well. I had already learned the hard way that electrolyte imbalance – caused by depleted quantities of vital minerals such as sodium, potassium and calcium – leads to cramp by hindering the muscle's ability to contract. Today I would be taking no chances.

Back at the foot of Truleigh Hill, though, my willpower was weakening. As I jogged laboriously back over the bridge and into the sixteenth mile, I felt spent. Into the hamlet of Annington and up the hill of the same name I trudged, my legs crying out for mercy. By now, I was eating into my spare tube of electrolytes, concocting my potions on the go in an increasingly desperate bid to keep moving. At the top of the hill, I swallowed my first gel – and came face to face with a vast field of feeding pigs.

This porcine metropolis belongs to Red Gate Farm, and it succeeded in momentarily taking my mind off my own travails. But two abortive attempts to start running again later, I was almost certain that my race was run and that I would have to pull out at Steyning Bowl. There was no shame, I told myself, in calling it a day after eighteen miles. The alternative was surely purgatory, capped by near-certain physical collapse.

My last throw of the dice was a potently minty protein ball, washed down with yet more glugs of electrolyte drink, which by now was beginning to taste foul. After falling into step with someone in a similarly crestfallen state, I gingerly joined him in an experimental jog to the aid station at Steyning Bowl. Remarkably, my legs barely murmured in protest. Perhaps

Family encouragement: my niece Ellame claps me on at the 15-mile stage.

there was life in them yet. Besides, didn't I owe it to myself to try to finish one of these things?

My new friend and I then trotted the next three miles to Chanctonbury Ring in the company of one of his running mates. Walking the bulk of a six-mile stretch of an ultra-marathon may sound like failure to the uninitiated; but when heroism risks costing you a finisher's medal, it comes to feel like common sense.

What's more, I was beginning to understand the psychological boost of familiarity. On the walk to the Ring (the third fort, in case you were wondering), it would have been easy to despair of ever reaching the finish line. What saved me from growing maudlin and losing my private mental battle was my ability to latch on to landmarks – bends in the path, clumps of trees, folds in the hillside – that I had spotted on previous runs along this stretch of downland (both of which are documented earlier in this book). 'Not far now' became my mantra.

I wasn't the only one trying to keep my mind occupied. One man, deep in the throes of another race, ran past in the opposite direction loudly singing Jingle Bells. The grimly focussed look on his face as he passed by was jarringly, if tellingly, at odds with the jaunty lyrics.

The Ring – and its amply stocked aid station – brought fresh impetus, and I was running again, downhill as far as the foot of Cissbury and 22.8 miles. (Believe me, those decimal points matter when you are out on your feet.) At the top of the gradually uncoiling path, I was off and running again, passing two mangled animal corpses en route to a rendezvous with family in the car park immediately to the west of Cissbury.

I had met my half-sister and niece on the river path back at mile fifteen, but this time the welcome party had swelled to three times that size. My ten-year-old nephew joined me for the remaining two miles of mingled disbelief and pride as the longest twelve miles of my running career ended, improbably, where it was always supposed to. On the finish line.

Right: nephew Arthur and his little sister Frankie join me on the track to Cissbury Ring. Arthur would accompany me for the last two miles down the hill to the finishing line.

Below: The longest twelve miles of my running career culminate under the Three Forts arch.

Journey's end!

Twelve Sussex downland runs

In approximate chronological order

The Hangover 5
Organised by Goring Road Runners each New Year's Day

The Steyning Stinger
Steyning AC

The Moyleman
Themoyleman.com

Jog Shop 20
The Jog Shop

The Three Forts Challenge
Worthing & District Rotary Clubs

Seaford Half Marathon
Newhaven, Peacehaven & Seaford Lions Club/Seaford Striders

Arun River Marathon
Sussex Trail Events

Round Hill Romp
Steyning AC

13 The Hard Way
Sussex Trail Events

Lewes Downland 10
Lewes AC

Beachy Head marathon
Eastbourne Borough Council

The Mince Pie 10
Seaford Striders

Sussex running clubs

Take your pick from the 38 running clubs affiliated to the Sussex County Athletics Association.

Arena 80 AC (Brighton & Hove)
arena80ac@hotmail.co.uk

Arunners (Littlehampton)
philmcerlain@hotmail.com

Bexhill Runners & Triathletes
gill@bexhillrunnerstriathletes.co.uk

Bodyworks XTC (Eastbourne)
yvettextc@live.co.uk

Brighton & Hove City AC
info@mphc.co.uk

Brighton & Hove Women's Running Club
nic@baxter.org

Brighton Tri Club
rpthorpe@hotmail.com

Burgess Hill Runners
bhrmemsec@gmail.com

Chichester Runners & AC
philbaker5@btinternet.com

Crawley AC
club@crawleyac.org.uk

Crawley Saints and Sinners
staceybuche@hotmail.co.uk

Crowborough Runners
ronnie.cutbill@btinternet.com

East Grinstead & District AC
mary.lordfamily@gmail.com

Eastbourne Rovers AC
chris@sussexbarn.com

Fittleworth Flyers
secretary@fittleworthflyers.org.uk

Hailsham Harriers
membership@hailsham-harriers.org.uk

Hastings AC
stephmccleery@hotmail.com

Hastings Runners
leesteph.runners@yahoo.com

Haywards Heath Harriers
membership@haywardsheath-harriers.co.uk

Heathfield Road Runners
info@heathfieldroadrunners.com

Henfield Joggers
enquiries@henfieldjoggers.co.uk

Horsham Blue Star Harriers
iancribb123@btinternet.com

Horsham Joggers
suesimmons99@hotmail.com

Lancing Eagles
davidclubb@sky.com

Lewes AC
membership@lewesac.co.uk

Mel's Milers (Horsham)
info@melsmilers.co.uk

Midhurst Milers Running Club
info@midhurstmilers.co.uk

Phoenix AC (Brighton)
nerine.standen@gmail.com

Rotary Road Runners (Bognor)
rrr@bognorprom10k.org

Seaford Striders
info@seafordstriders.org.uk

Steyning AC
steyningac@gmail.com

Tone Zone Runners (Bognor Regis)
membership@tonezonerunners.org

Team Synergy (Worthing)
chrissmarsden@aol.com

Tuff Fitty Triathlon Club (Littlehampton)
clive.harvey@tinyworld.co.uk

Uckfield Runners
utopiarunners@tiscali.co.uk

Wadhurst Runners
albertlkemp@btinternet.com

Worthing & District Harriers
gavin@runbase.co.uk

Worthing Striders
andrew.saych@sky.com

Index